Gathered Truths

Thoughtful Contemplation & Sacred Inquiry

Volume I

Copyright © 2019 by Jennifer Yockey

All rights reserved.

No part of this publication or the information in it may be quoted from or reproduced in any form by means such as printing, scanning, photocopying or otherwise without prior written permission of the copyright holder.

Cover Photo by Amber Linn Photography
Butterfly Cuff: @thecuffchic

ISBN: 9781090982636

TABLE OF CONTENTS

ACKNOWLEDGEMENTS 5

NEXT 7

RECEIVE 9

DREAM 11

CREATE 13

SACRED 15

NOURISH 17

RIGOROUS HONESTY 19

INQUIRY 21

PRESENCE & RESPONSE 23

CHEERLEADER 25

OBSERVE 27

HABIT 29

QUIT 31

RELEASE 33

ROOT 35

CONNECTION 37

BEAUTY 39

MIND TRICKS 41

EASE 43

HEALTH 45

PEACE 47

EQUANIMITY 49

EMOTIONS	51
STOP	53
WORTH	55
LOVE	57
FORGIVENESS	59
LISTEN	61
REFLECT	63
SAVASANA	65
INTERNAL PEACE	67
PRACTICE	69
RIGHTS	71
IMPERMANENCE	73
THROUGH	75
HEALING	77
CONTAINER	79
REGRETS	81
FEELINGS	83
LAZY	85
IMAGINE	87
WANT | NEED	89
THE PAST	91
LET GO	93
BE STILL	95
ABOUT THE AUTHOR	97

ACKNOWLEDGEMENTS

This book would never have come to fruition without the people in my life that believed in me when I didn't believe in myself. They are my faith keepers, cheerleaders, arse kickers and truth tellers.

Thank you:

Jay

Lucas

Mom

Dad

Ryan

Grandma

Coach Jennie

Anna

The Book Release Support Tribe

NEXT

"If you can see your path laid out in front of you step by step, you know it's not your path. Your own path you make with every step you take. That's why it's your path."
Joseph Campbell

Life situations can sometimes be daunting. They might be unfamiliar and you may not have any idea how to navigate them.

△

The reality is, that you can't possibly know how to handle *every* situation. How could you?

△

One rule that you *can* follow is to just take the next indicated step. One step at a time. The path will continue to reveal itself. People will meet you on the path to either direct you or thwart you. If you pay attention, you will find your way; over and over again.

△

You won't always know what to do. Take a deep breath. Make a decision to take a step. Sometimes that step will be forward and other times it will be backward, left or right.

Sometimes, the next step is the decision to not step at all.

RECEIVE

"Until we can receive with an open heart, we're never really giving with an open heart."
Brené Brown

Are you more comfortable giving than receiving? When someone is generous with you, whether it be time, attention or gifts, are you accepting or rigid? Do you find that you brush off compliments and re-direct the conversation? Do you notice your body tense and become rigid? Does your face flush?

∆

You aren't alone. Many of us are givers to the point of self-sacrifice. We use this benevolence to shield ourselves, to protect ourselves from really allowing ourselves to get close.
Our *giving* is our control.

∆

The next time someone gives you something; whether it be a compliment, hug or physical gift... be still. Let them say what they want and need to say. Receive the gift without re-direction. Pay attention to your body language and self-talk. Notice what your resistance is actually about.
Breathe and say: "thank you."

DREAM

"To accomplish great things, we must not only act, but also dream; not only plan but also believe."
Anatole France

When was the last time you dreamed? I mean, *really* thought about something totally outrageous to do; for your family, your business, your relationships, yourself.

△

As adults, we get so busy *doing*. We are on to the next task, the next thing on our "to do" list. Running from one thing to another without presence, attention or intention.

△

Stop for a moment or a few moments and think about where you are in one aspect of your life. Then, **write down** the biggest dream for that part of your life. Make it **grand**.
And then compare the two.

△

Where are you now versus the dream? How far off are you? How does that make you feel?
What are you going to do about it?

CREATE

"Balance is not something you find but something you create."
Jana Kingsford

Relationships, children, career, dogs, extended family, laundry, garbage day, grocery shopping, house maintenance, bills, daily choices and decisions… **a d u l t i n g.**

∆

It's a lot, isn't it? And you can add to the pile when someone is sick or the kids aren't in school or you are a single parent.

∆

What I know for sure is that balance is **created**. We need to attempt to create and carve out space for ourselves or we will burn out. Sometimes burnout looks like the flu, a nagging pain in your back, a short temper or over eating/shopping/drinking.

∆

Put your oxygen mask on first. It doesn't mean a week on the Amalfi Coast (although that sounds nice). It means a walk around the block with no phone, reading a chapter in a book or five minutes just choosing to focus on your breathing.

∆

How will you create space and balance for yourself today?

SACRED

"Sacred Space is time and space we set aside, or which spontaneously arises, to experience a depth, richness, and sense of meaning that usually escapes us in fast-paced everyday life when we are not as connected as we could be with our body, intuition, good thinking, compassion and empathy, and other emotions."
Adam Weber

Do you have a sacred space?
Do you have a place to go to in order to find the ground?
To connect with yourself?
To check-in with how things are going with **you**?

∆

I have a little corner in my bedroom with sage, chakra stones, a daily reflection book, a succulent and a salt rock lamp.
I think I will move it today… to a more prominent place.

∆

What will you create?
What will it include?
When will you do it?

NOURISH

"And now I will do what is best for me..."
unknown

What can you do *today* to clear your mind, strengthen your body and nourish your soul?
When was the last time you even asked yourself those questions?

△

Even though I have a lot of tools and information at my disposal, I still tend to burn the candle at both ends, not listen to my body, put off self-care...and then my body says "NO".

△

It is best to have continual maintenance. Just like a car, if we keep it fueled and get a checkup every 10,000 miles, the car stays in good shape and runs smoothly. Waiting until we are on the side of the road with a burned up engine or out of gas is never good. This same principle applies to us; not just to our bodies but our mind, heart and spirit, too.

△

So, what are **you** going to do today for *maintenance*?

RIGOROUS HONESTY

"Wearing a mask wears you out. Faking it is fatiguing. The most exhausting activity is pretending to be what you know you aren't."
Rick Warren

Being authentically ourselves is sometimes scary. What if we are rejected? What if we are not liked? What will people say?

∆

Have you had any of those thoughts? They aren't uncommon. At the end of the day, we all want to be *"part of"*. We want to be accepted and liked. We want community and a tribe and we want to fit in.

∆

Want to know a secret? If you don't tell yourself the truth, if you don't find peace and acceptance with who you are, you will *always* have those thoughts.

∆

The Buddha teaches that what someone else thinks of us is none of our business. Additionally, it is important to be ok with *what is* as well as who and what we are; in the present moment and as we evolve.

∆

When we hold on to secrets, when we have awful and toxic self- talk, when we don't walk our talk...that is when we are most vulnerable to others' opinions about who we are.

∆

Let's get our side of the street clean. Tell the truth. Write it down, talk to a trusted friend or therapist or doctor. Say it all. Let it go. And then notice how your perspective changes. *Notice the empowerment that occurs when you truly know who you are and when there is nothing to hide.*

INQUIRY

"Freedom worships inquiry."
Danielle LaPorte

I teach a lot of classes that combine movement and internal inquiry. My own experience, as well as my student's, is that this can be uncomfortable at first and then...
complete freedom.

∆

Taking a look inside ourselves and deciding to repair the past so that we can create space for a healthy present is not always *fun*. But once we get through the muck and find resolution, there is relief, space, forgiveness and new possibilites.

∆

There is freedom in the truth.

∆

What "thing" is lurking?
What are you continually trying to shove back down,
deny or ignore?

∆

Maybe it's time to inquire, to look within... I am guessing that there is no boogie man under the bed.
It may be a bit painful and you might not like it, but you aren't going to die from the truth.

PRESENCE & RESPONSE

"Compassion can be described as letting ourselves be touched by the vulnerability and suffering that is within ourselves and all beings. The full flowering of compassion also includes action: Not only do we attune to the presence of suffering, we respond to it."
Tara Brach

It happens to all of us; **loss**. The details might be different, but the end result is the same. Loss of a child, a pet, a dream, a spouse, a job, a lover or time.

∆

There are grief cycles. They aren't things we master but are stops along a journey that wind and turn. The intensity of the cycle will lessen over time but we will re-visit the cycle when memories, a particular scent, a song or event reminds us.

∆

You cannot push through. Grief doesn't work that way. You cannot gut it out, push it down, deny it or think that you can keep it at bay. Recognize what it is. Cry and shout. Breathe. Say what needs to be said. Shed the tears that want to be shed. Be gentle, kind, understanding and compassionate with yourself.

∆

Be present with all of it. Respond as needed. Reach out for help.

∆

Inhale | Exhale | Repeat

CHEERLEADER

"If you are looking for a hobby or a vocation, become a cheerleader. There are enough critics. Cheerlead for yourself, your immediate circle of influence, your community."
Jay Keel

Wouldn't it be great if a marching band and cheer squad followed you around for a day?!? Are you smiling right now just thinking of it? You drop your kids off at school and the band and cheer squad celebrate you. You remember the paper towels at the grocery store and there they are at the check-out line. You climb into bed without raising your voice at the kids or husband... and on cue, they break out in song and cartwheels.

Δ

Just take a moment to visualize that. How would that make you feel? What does the smile feel like across your face? Does your heart open? Do your eyes smile, too? Imagine your child or someone that you really love. Imagine the band and cheer squad following *them* around. Can you imagine how that would make them feel or the people around them? What about their teachers, the janitor, the check-out clerks at the grocery store, the barista?

Δ

The combination of visualization and action are so powerful. We probably can't get the cheer squad and college band to follow us around, but we can visualize what it would feel like if we were celebrated and applauded all day rather than criticized.

Δ

Start with yourself. Then your family. Then your co-workers. Then the people that you don't really know. Then the people that you have resentments against or less love for.
See what happens. See how your daily outlook changes.

OBSERVE

"The act of watching ourselves, neutrally observing ourselves without judgement or reproach, can be a powerful tool for change."
Melodie Beattie

Watching ourselves is a practice. It's a practice that is never ending and is not meant to be mastered. It is a journey, an evolution, a path that we walk as we change throughout our lives and encounter situations or patterns that need to evolve or be released.

△

Perhaps you have tried to make a change recently. Maybe you have read books, researched and analyzed and have not had success.

△

For today, just observe.
How do you act?
Do you react or respond?
How do you feel?
What things do you say out loud and to yourself?
Be kind. Be neutral. Don't judge. Just observe.

△

What did you notice?
What are your observations?
Keep doing it.
Keep witnessing.

HABIT

"On average, it takes more than two months before a new behavior becomes automatic — 66 days to be exact. And how long it takes a new habit to form can vary widely depending on the behavior, the person, and the circumstances."
James Clear

The 21 days to change a habit rule is a myth. So, let's stop beating ourselves up when we revert back to old patterns or habits.
Get back on the horse and try again.

Δ

And let's be honest, the thing you want to change, just didn't **happen**. You didn't wake up this morning with 20 extra pounds. You didn't spontaneously start yelling at your kids. And that two hours that you spend at night getting lost in the rabbit hole of social media? It was never your intention. But here we are.

Δ

Building habits, come to find out, is NOT an **all or nothing** proposition. If you mess up, it doesn't erase all the time you have built changing. **Disclaimer:** The harsh reality with regards to drugs and alcohol is that one slip up can lead to catastrophic results…However, you still do not lose the time you have accumulated or the knowledge/coping skills you have attained.

Δ

So, what are you wanting to change? What rut have you got yourself stuck in? What is today's date? If you create a plan and create accountability, you will be well on your way in 66 days. This should be a **RELIEF** to know that it takes time. Be patient with yourself.
Do some research; ask for help, make a plan.

QUIT

"Be A Quitter. Quit. Quit abusive relationships. Quit. Quit toxic friendships. Quit. Quit people who pull you down. Quit. Quit habits that cause you harm. Quit. Quit. Quit while you still can."
Nandhitha Hariharan

Five things you should quit today:
comparison
people pleasing
negative self- talk
re-living the past
future tripping

Δ

I think that it is fair to say that we have all experienced the above list at some time in our lives. Hopefully, we recognize that there is zero upside to practicing any of them.

Δ

When you notice yourself participating in the above list, be aware of how it makes you feel. Where do you feel sensation in your body? Is your stomach in knots, do you have a twitch in your eye, are your neck and shoulders tight, your lower back?

Δ

Your body holds the key to the root cause of these feelings: boundaries crossed or never set, not being able to speak your truth, fear of not belonging or not being heard or seen.

Δ

Take note. *What is really going on?*

RELEASE

"Writing is a form of therapy. Sometimes I wonder how all those who do not write, compose, or paint can manage to escape the madness, melancholia, the panic and fear which is inherent in a human situation."
Graham Greene

Life happens. Challenges arise. Depending on your life circumstances, you might have **A LOT** of balls in the air. Finding a healthy way to decompress throughout the day and/or at the end of the day helps with sleep as well as the ability to organize and process.

∆

Writing is powerful. It allows all that is *living on the inside of you* to reside on the outside. Grinding it out in our heads is typically a recipe for disaster as our minds like to keep us safe and send us messages of worse-case scenarios that are not necessarily accurate.

∆

Set a timer. Write, without a filter, for 10 minutes in the morning and 10 minutes at night. If you can only manage one of those, then do that. Don't let the suggestion of time stop you. Get a pretty journal or grab some scrap paper and write.

∆

Take notice of how you feel emotionally and physically before you start. Take notice of how you feel when you finish.

ROOT

"Long-lasting change that will help you create new habits and actions requires an inside-out approach, as well as two very important tools: the mirror and time."
Darren L. Johnson

Getting to the root cause of why we do the things we do is an integral part of change. Rarely is there a quick fix. Reading books, trying new methods and joining new groups is helpful and important but more than likely your behavior
will return to the old.
This is not BAD news!

Δ

Getting to the root cause allows us to create new patterns and new brain pathways to create lasting change. If we know **WHY** we do something (the **thing** that sets us off to do the action), then we can find **other** actions when that **thing** sets us off.

Δ

What I know for sure is that *we don't think our way to right action, we act our way to right thinking.*

Δ

For today, when you **FEEL** like you are going to do the thing you don't want to do: drink, over eat, yell at your kids... **PAUSE**. Take a deep breath and notice what is happening and perhaps why you are wanting to do that **thing**.

Δ

And then let's consider doing something else.

CONNECTION

"To lose our connection with the body is to become spiritually homeless. Without an anchor we float aimlessly, battered by the winds and waves of life."
Anodea Judith

In workshops that I teach we often talk about the sensations/feelings/pain that we have in our bodies and how most days, we just push through and ignore it...until our bodies finally say NO.

Δ

We talk about staying with the sensation in the different yoga poses we do; following the sensation, noticing the sensation. We named the sensation and gave it a color, too. And then we discussed what the cure might be. The entire exercise is to provide a path to connection rather than disassociation.

Δ

Today, pay attention to your body. It does so much for you each and every day. Pay attention to how you talk to it, what you feed it, how you nurture it. Perhaps, the aches and pains
are a directional sign.

Δ

Before your body goes to FULL STOP: connect and listen.

BEAUTY

"To be beautiful means to be yourself. You don't need to be accepted by others. You need to accept yourself."
Thich Nhat Hanh

What one thing are you self-conscious about?

△

Let's highlight it as a strength today. Recognize its importance in the way it has shaped you and perhaps continues to shape you.

△

How does it feel in your body and heart to acknowledge that **thing** that has been so heavy and dark, is actually **your superpower**?

△

Do a little writing or even speaking in to your voice recorder. What if this thing that holds so much shame and embarrassment was actually not yours but your daughter's or best friend's? What advice or compassion would you offer them? What words would you use? What tone would you use?

△

Try using the same tone, the same words,
the same compassion with yourself.

MIND TRICKS

"Impulse and Awareness cannot co-exist."
Jen Yockey

Think about it. Think about it with regards to online shopping, alcohol, french fries, raising your voice...

△

Once you bring awareness to the **thing**...
impulse/compulsion cannot exist.

△

Internal inquiry is powerful. Awareness is transformative.

△

You can still make the decision to drink, eat the fries and raise your voice, but it becomes a *conscious decision rather than an impulse.*

△

The goal is to create space between stimulus and response. That is where the power and freedom lies.

△

Reactions are different than responses. Impulsive behavior is different than conscious, intentional decision making.

△

Pause. Witness. Assess. Respond.

EASE

"Being at ease with the unknown is crucial for
answers to come to you."
Eckhart Tolle

Being at ease, cultivating ease is not always **EASY**.

△

To find ease in the unknown, to trust, to accept, to let go…
is a practice.

△

From personal experience, however, I can tell you that stillness, ease and acceptance create space for new thoughts, ideas, as well as room to breathe and grow.

△

Where are you wanting more ease?
Where do you feel resistance?
What are you considering letting go of?
What part of your life do you crave more **space?**

HEALTH

"Health does not always come from medicine. Most of the time it comes from peace of mind, peace in the heart, peace in the soul. It comes from laughter and love."
Unknown

Where are you aching today?
Does your heart hurt?
Your neck?
Your shoulders?
Your hips?
Your stomach?

∆

Can you take five minutes for yourself?
Can you laugh with a trusted friend?
Can you send an email to someone that you love?
Can you write, **unfiltered**, tonight?

∆

Sometimes we are SO in the middle of the muck that we don't know what we need. If that is you right now, that is ok. Write about *that*. Be **honest** about that. **Honor** that.

PEACE

"When we make peace with our past, we create room in our present for positive change, choice and growth."
Jen Yockey

We have all done things, that after some introspection, we wish we hadn't.

△

We have, in some instances, been treated horribly.
We have experienced trauma and pain.
We have tried to find blame and played the victim... all to the detriment of our current and future selves.

△

Time to make peace. Time to let go of and heal what is no longer serving us. *Ready?*

△

Awareness
Willingness
Acceptance
Action
Change
Freedom

EQUANIMITY

/ekwəˈnimədē/:: finding a steadiness, composure and evenness within the roller coaster of emotions; joy, sadness, bargaining, grief, anger.

Written in the Spring of 2018; RIP Sweet Atlas

△

Our big dog, Atlas, is having a good day; acting like he did before the cancer diagnosis. This brings me joy. We have an oncology appointment today. I am grateful for the money to pay for it and for my friends that were able to recommend a place to go. I am breathing through the fact that he won't be with us for another five years. I am present with him now.
I am attempting to set an example for my son.

△

Acceptance does not mean approval.

△

What are you dealing with today?
How can you create the steadiness and composure that you need?
How can you be an example to your child, partner, friends or circle of influence?
How can you authentically show up for yourself?

EMOTIONS

"Rigid denial of our emotions just doesn't work—not for individuals, families, societies, or our planet."
Susan David

Emotions. They exhaust me. I spent so many years trying not to have them, that now, they can seem so intense.

△

Death is part of life. None of us will escape this reality. Grief is real. There is no pushing through... *more like riding the wave of it.*

△

Death is not the only form of loss; Divorce, Time, Dreams, Faith, Yourself, Finances, Memories...

△

On repeat today: *Emotions are meant to be felt... Not fixed.*

△

When was the last time that you identified your emotions?
When was the last time you let yourself have them?
Are you able to let other people have theirs?

STOP

"Happiness cannot be traveled to, owned, earned, worn or consumed. Happiness is the spiritual experience of living every minute with love, grace, and gratitude."
Denis Waitley

STOP what you are doing right now.

△

Look around and acknowledge:
FIVE things that you **see**.
FOUR things that you can **touch**.
THREE things that you can **hear**.
TWO things that you can **taste**.
ONE thing that you can **smell**.

△

How does your body feel?
Notice your emotional/mental state.

△

Close your eyes. Hands on your heart center.
Smile and take 3 cleansing breaths.

WORTH

"You are imperfect, you are wired for struggle, but you are worthy of love and belonging."
Brené Brown

I distinctly remember the day that I shouted: *"At what point did I decide that I was not worthy; worthy of love, worthy of respect, worthy of peace, joy, my truth, my own power?"*

△

I recently wrote a letter to my 10-year-old self.
(This was the time that I remember feeling helpless & powerless.)

△

I let her know that she would be ok but that it wasn't ok to be bullied, to be chased, to be pinched and poked. I let her know that she was safe, seen and heard.
Writing is powerful.
Forgiveness is powerful.
Awareness is powerful.

△

What would you let your 10-year-old self know?
What do you think she needs to hear?
What would make her feel safe and empowered?

LOVE

"There is so much love in your heart,
you should give some to yourself."
r.z.

Self- love. I remember how those words used to feel like a gut punch every time I heard them. I had such disdain for myself. It was as if I were two different people. The one that I showed the world and the one that I *knew*.
I am grateful today as my insides match my outsides…
most of the time.

Δ

How do you show yourself love?
How do you express self-compassion?
How do you impart grace and self-understanding?

Δ

It's ok to not know.
It is also ok to start asking some questions and get curious about your own mental wellness.

Δ

Sometimes it is easier to think about how we would treat/love a best friend and *then attempt to treat ourselves the same way.*

FORGIVENESS

"The only way to learn forgiveness is to be betrayed. You might understand the intellectual concept of forgiveness, but you will only learn how to truly forgive when someone has done something that requires you to love them and let it go. Life demands these hurtful experiences for you to learn how forgiveness feels, it could be no other way. If there is anyone in your life that you must forgive, instead of seeing them as someone who has hurt you, try to see them as someone who was sent to teach you forgiveness and thank them for this precious gift – then forgive them, and let it go."
Jackson Kiddard

Perhaps the person that needs the forgiveness is *you*.

∆

All the soul searching and introspection that you have been doing... it hasn't only brought you growth and perspective but has brought you to **here**; to the crossroads of forgiveness or continued self- deprecation.

∆

What will you choose?
How free do you want to be?

∆

Perhaps start with the following mantra:
I forgive you
Please forgive me
I forgive myself

LISTEN

"Listen. Are you breathing just a little bit and calling it a life?"
Mary Oliver

What *one action* can you take today that will move you in the direction of a dream/want/goal?

Δ

Perhaps the first step is just actually setting a goal or considering what you desire; maybe you haven't done that in a while.

Δ

Maybe it is cleaning out the refrigerator or your closet.
Maybe it is looking for another job or considering a new career.
Maybe it's time to invest in yourself; join a group, take a class, enroll in school.

Δ

What do you really want out of this great, big, beautiful life?
What are you waiting for?
What step will you take next?

REFLECT

"My outer experiences are a reflection of my internal condition."
Gabrielle Bernstein

Sometimes I don't want to embrace this. Sometimes, it seems easier to blame the outside, blame others.
However, there is no freedom or relief until I look within.

△

Evolving and growing is difficult but rewarding work.

△

Who or what are you blaming?
What would happen if you took- a -peek within?

△

Where do you want to grow and evolve?
How is blaming other people and things holding you back?

△

What is your part?

SAVASANA

"Breathe.
Slowly.
Soften.
With Ease."
Unknown

If you were to describe how you want your day to day life to feel…
What would that **look** like?
What would it **feel** like?
What would it **taste** and **sound** like?

∆

For me, I like Sundays to feel like savasana.
I try to cultivate ease, stillness, comfort and peace.

∆

Monday through Saturday? I am working on it.

∆

Where are you most at ease?
When are you most at ease?
What part of those places can you cultivate / re-create in your every day life?

INTERNAL PEACE

"Peace of mind is not the absence of conflict from life, but the
ability to cope with it."
Unknown

For many years, I was under the assumption that if I was going to
be peaceful internally, *all the things* had to be in perfect order; the
marriage, the friends, my weight, my complexion,
my job, my home…

∆

Today I realize that within the chaos of life, there is peace. Just as
in the eye of the hurricane, there is stillness.

∆

You don't need a quiet space and an hour to find internal peace.
You can take intentional breaths, place your hand on your heart
and create peace standing in the middle of the grocery store.

∆

My biggest "aha!"?:
Mindfulness and the creation of internal peace is a practice.
Mastery is not necessary nor is it the goal.

PRACTICE

"Practice doesn't make perfect, it makes *better*."
Lucas Keel, 6

Six- year-olds have **a LOT** of profound thoughts. Sometimes they are about dinosaurs and legos and sometimes they are about life.

△

Yoga teaches me much about practice, awareness and betterment **for that particular day.** My body feels different day to day. Some nights I sleep really well and others, not so much. Some days I eat nutritious foods and skip the caffeine and somedays it's almonds and americanos.

△

I am different every day. My practice of **ALL** things each day is different because *I am different*. There is grace and kindness in just practicing for betterment rather than mastery.

△

Where can you practice today… for betterment rather than mastery?

RIGHTS

"You have the inalienable right to take up space."
Jen Yockey

Not only do you have the **right** but you **deserve** to
and are **worthy** of it.

△

Do you find yourself shrinking a little and dimming your light a bit around some people and situations?
Do you temper your opinions and fail to ask for what you really want for fear of being a burden or ostracized?

△

What if, just for today, you didn't do any of that?
What if you believed with your WHOLE heart that you had the right to take up space?

△

How would your day go?
What would it look like?
How would you feel?
What would you do?

IMPERMANENCE

"To put it concisely, we suffer when we resist the noble and irrefutable truth of impermanence and death."
Pema Chödrön

Impermanence. It's a difficult one to get your head around. It is easier to stomach when we are the observer rather than the one experiencing it.

△

What situation is causing you suffering right now?
Can you sit with it rather than resisting it?
You can resist it, again, in a minute or two.
But for now, just sit with it.

△

Is there Peace within you when you don't resist?
Are there other situations that you are resisting?
I know that you can feel it. It's that pit in your stomach, the tension in your face, the tightness in the shoulders.

△

What would it look like if you just let it be?
What would you gain?
What are your **perceived** losses?

THROUGH

"They tried to bury us, they didn't know we were seeds."
Dinos Christianopolous

That *thing* that you are going through today? Not pleasant, *at all*. I get it. It might be a person, a place, a thing...whatever it is, you will get through it. You will grow and bloom. You will thrive.

△

And all of the growing and blooming doesn't take away the hurt, the pain, the disappointment, the betrayal, the loss. There will be a scar. There will be memories. There will be tears, anger and frustration. *Let it come.* ***Let it all come.***

△

All of it is prepping the soil for growth and beauty. I realize that you cannot see it right now. It is not a fast process. Sometimes it goes so slow, you don't even realize there *is* a process.

△

Deep breath.

△

Right now, it's like this.

HEALING

"A healer does not heal you. A healer is someone who holds space
for you while you awaken your inner healer,
so that you may heal yourself."
Maryam Hasnaa

I do. You do. We do.

△

We heal from broken hearts, divorce, health issues, trauma,
betrayal, disappointment, and loss of *all kinds*.

△

That healing doesn't mean we skip the painful parts. Healing sometimes hurts. There is a process that happens when a wound heals. We can't make it go faster, even though we would like to.

△

There is learning within the healing. We learn patience and self-compassion. We learn how strong and powerful we truly are.
We can learn much, if we allow for it.

△

Find the ground. Confide in a trusted companion. Lean on your
faith or something greater than you.
Talk with a therapist, hire a coach,
speak with your pastor or priest.

△

*You have all you need inside of you, sometimes
we just need help re-discovering it.*

CONTAINER

"It is mental slavery to cling to things that have stopped serving its purpose in your life."
Chinonye J. Chidolue

Throughout life, we put *things* in this "container": hopes, dreams, goals, responsibilities, values, thoughts, ideals...
And just like our junk drawer, it gets full and not attended to.

△

When was the last time you took inventory of your container?
Do you like what is in it?
If not, how will you transform your container to make it look like the one you want?

△

What is in your container?
What needs to be removed?
What do you want in there?
How does it feel (in your body) when you think about cleaning it out?
What does your mind have to say about the idea of cleaning it out and creating space?

REGRETS

"Don't regret the past, Learn from it."
Unknown

Lessons learned. Mistakes made. Yesterdays.

△

Let it all go:
the disappointment
how it should have been
the shame
the poor decision
the guilt
the relationship
the job

△

Whether you have TEN or ONE to let go of… do it.
Because when you do, you create space for what will be.

△

If you don't want to right now, that's ok.
But perhaps, you ask "why not?"

△

Why don't I want to let it go?
Why do I want to hold on to it?
What do I feel when I consider letting it go?
What would REALLY happen if I did?

FEELINGS

Feelings Come
Feelings Go
Feelings Come
Feelings Go
Feelings Come
Feelings Go
Let them.

What if we just *let* our emotions come and go?
What if we just *observed* the process of our
emotions arising and dissipating?
What if we *witnessed* our emotions rather than reacted to them?
What if we *accepted* that emotions are directional signs?

∆

What would shift for you?
What if you believed that feelings and emotions were just part of the human experience?
Who would you be if you just felt your feelings rather than judged them?

∆

Grab your journal. Set a timer for 11 minutes.
Write.
No filter.
Just write.

LAZY

"Thoughts have energy. Make sure your thoughts
are positive and powerful."
Anonymous

When you read or hear the word *lazy*, what is your response?

∆

Rest is not lazy.
Sitting down to gather yourself is not lazy.
Closing your eyes for 15 minutes or 3 hours is not lazy.
Taking the day off isn't lazy.
Self-care is not lazy.
Putting your jammies on at 7pm is not lazy.
Taking a break is not lazy.
You are not lazy.

∆

Webster's Dictionary definition of lazy is:
la·zy
ˈlāzē/
adjective
1.**unwilling** to work or use energy.

∆

How does that definition feel to you?
Does it shift something within you?
Does it give you permission to sit, lie down or get your jammies on?

IMAGINE

"The best use of imagination is creativity. The worst use of imagination is anxiety."
Deepak Chopra

When was the last time you day dreamed?
When was the last time you actually sat
still long enough to imagine?
Does it make you uncomfortable to be still?
Does it make you uncomfortable to be with your own thoughts?
Does stillness encourage creativity or anxiety?

∆

Inquiry is a practice.
Inquiry encourages us to be more flexible and pliable.
Our edges become softer.
Our answers more expansive.

∆

Do not be fearful of the questions… or the answers.

WANT | NEED

"You can never get enough of what you don't need, because what you don't need won't satisfy you."
Dallin H. Oaks

Oh boy. That's a doozy. Right?!?

△

How many different things can *that* apply to?
Booze, sex with people you don't know, gambling, sugar, shopping, social media.

△

Sometimes the thing that we think we absolutely **need** is not what we **want** at all. We want the anxiety and uncomfortable-ness to go away. And so, we get online and put 13 things in our shopping cart to numb out. We click **BUY NOW** and maybe, for a brief moment, we weren't thinking about the stressful things...but we weren't finding a solution either. And **now** we are not only stressed about the first thing but also the bill we just created by binge shopping.

△

Then, the shame kicks in. (just what we need: self-loathing.)

△

This vicious cycle is no fun. It's not fun for us, our families or friends. It's not fun for our colleagues or clients either.

△

So, let's find some healthy responses to stress **and** get to the root cause of our stressors, too.

△

Let's also remember that if you are breathing, you are going to experience life and have emotions. It's called LIVING.

THE PAST

"Yesterday is gone. Tomorrow has not yet come.
We have only today. Let us begin."
—Mother Theresa

Nothing in your past has power over you now. Nothing.

∆

Can you consider this as a possibility?
Do you already believe this?
What belief would you have to release in order to consider this?
What would change if you started living as if this was true?

∆

Taking momentary trips down memory lane in order to reflect and grow is healthy. Deciding to unpack your bags and STAY in the past creates problems in our present.

∆

Take a moment to reflect.
Grab your journal.
Write about the memory.
Give yourself 10 or 15 minutes.

∆

Come back to the **here and now**. List five things (out loud) that you can see and 4 things that you can touch.

Welcome back.

LET GO

"Lose your mind. Find your Soul."
Unknown

What if you let it all go?

△

Who would you be without the judgement?
How would you feel if you just observed your thoughts rather than reacted to them?
What would happen if the drama and chaos faded away?
How would you feel if you completely trusted your own intuition?

△

Sometimes the stories we convince ourselves of aren't even true.
They aren't factually based.
They are fears or anxieties of the past.
They are worst case scenarios.

△

Peace is possible.
Responding rather than reacting, is possible.
Trust is possible.
Freedom and relief are possible.

△

You are in charge.

BE STILL

"Sometimes finding that quiet stillness within us
is our highest and greatest aspiration."
Unknown

When was the last time you just stood still?

∆

Try it. Set a timer for two minutes.
Take your shoes off and just stand.

∆

Notice the ground beneath your feet.
Place your right hand on your heart and feel your chest
rise and fall as you breathe.
Observe your body. How does it feel?
Observe your thoughts. Are they positive?
Negative? Supportive? Judgmental?
Observe your mental state.
How are you feeling today?

∆

You don't have to do anything about what you find.
Just notice.
Keep noticing.
Keep connecting.

ABOUT THE AUTHOR

Jen lives in the beautiful Coachella Valley with her husband, son and an array of super pampered rescue dogs.

When she isn't writing and gathering women together to create sacred bonds with themselves and others, she is dreaming of the sea and planning her next adventure.

Find her at:

https://www.instagram.com/jen.yockey/
https://www.facebook.com/jenlyockey/
https://www.jenyockey.com

Made in the USA
Middletown, DE
16 August 2020

15439999R00059